Broken Vessel
(Letters to Abba)

By

Latoya Washington

Broken Vessels - Letters to Abba

Published in the United States of America by Latoya Washington.

 Scriptures are taken from the **Holy Bible, The King James Version** unless otherwise marked.

ISBN - 978-0-692-72947-2

Printed in the United States of America

July 2020

Dedication

This book is dedicated to the down-casted, overlooked, abused, mistreated, neglected, betrayed, homeless, hurt and wounded people. I am a witness that God does not despise a broken spirit or a contrite heart (Psalms 51:17). God is able to purify, refine and define who you are. He is able to use the broken pieces of our lives and mold us into beautiful broken vessels!

Table of Contents

Additional Poems From The Heart

#RealTalk Intimate conversation between Father and daughter

Foreword

I'm honored to discuss my reflections of the essence of reading writings of Latoya Washington. Her ability to paint morals of imaginary, clarity, feelings, and emotions with her strokes of the pen is amazing. You will be taken on a stimulating ride for your mind, where you will be at ease while Latoya's creativity will guide you through Reading her writings is truly a time not wasted, it's a positive moment of time that will comfort your mind. Words cannot fully express this book but experiencing it will. So, I recommend everyone to invest your time to read her writings; it will touch your heart.

Another bonus to her writings was the after effect; you will be drawn to read it multiple times, to savor all the flavors. You can tell from her expression that she defiantly has a wide background in many writing styles. Her writing style is like a gumbo with multiple flavors, that sends pleasure to all your taste buds, that all would love to indulge in, and it's uniquely original. Latoya has a down to earth essence that lingers in her writings while having a timeless relativity in her work, that shines through the after taste once you are finished reading the book.

Honestly, without being bias, this poetry book is designed with in mind, and I can assure you that you will be blessed by every page.

David Washington
Rhema Creationz
CEO/Founder

Acknowledgement

I want to first acknowledge my Lord, Savior, King, Friend and first love Jesus Christ. It has been years in the making to develop the person I am today. It was your love that was obedient unto death that was shown on Calvary, that I am here today. Secondly to my husband, best friend, confidant, mirror and love. You have pulled out areas in me that I didn't see in myself. Since we reunited after fifteen years, my love continues to progress. I love you David Schyler Washington to the moon and beyond. Lastly I want to acknowledge my mother Veeta Bonner and step-father Jimmie Bonner. Even through all the obstacles I look back over my life and know that God has always been in control. To my sisters, brothers, nieces, nephews and family. Please know that I love you and God deserves the glory for His rich mercies towards us.

Introduction

This book is designed to edify, educate and encourage every reader. Writing poetry is a gift given to me by the Lord and as you read each page of writing, it is my prayer that you are truly blessed and you will be able to see you in this poetry collection.

Thank you for your purchase and I am praying that you will be blessed and satisfied as you read each page.

Get ready to be blessed…

Quit Girl

They told me to quit girl

Just give up on this dream girl

You aren't built for this stage girl

This here is too big for your britches girl

These shoes are too big for your feet girl

You are not qualified for this thing girl

You are not experienced for this stage girl

You are not ready for this thing girl

But hearing the whispers of the naysayers

I still go, Holy Spirit says go!

My Father in Heaven says it's so

Jesus is with me, so I'll go!

They told me to quit girl

What could you possibly learn from this girl?

You should be this and should be that girl

You can't have it, just give up and quit girl

Placed obstacles in my path, so go head and faint, just quit girl

These shoes are just too big for your feet girl

Those britches are just too big for your waist girl

But still I go, Holy Spirit says go!

My Father in Heaven say's it's time, so let's go

Jesus is with me, so I'll go!

Instead of quitting, I will press on!

Fight on

Be strong

Because, I have never been a give up and quit girl!

Stirring

I can feel you

Stirring in the atmosphere

I can feel you

Moving in the atmosphere

Heaven is coming and Heaven is drawing near

I can feel you, time is drawing near

The Spirit of God is moving

The Spirit of God is shaking the earth

Can you feel the trembling? Can you feel the stirring?

The Angels are singing, proclaiming Jesus is Lord

Holy, Holy, Lord God Almighty they declare and my soul cries out Oh Lord

I can feel you

Stirring in the atmosphere

I can feel you

Moving in the atmosphere

Heaven is coming

Sound the Alarm, they day of the Lord is drawing near

I can feel, your presence is felt

Trumpet is blowing, loud and clear

I can *feel* you

Your Spirit is stirring in the atmosphere

Heaven is coming, day *of* the Lord is drawing near

Promise Land

Yeah

Take me to the Promise land

Trees green

Prosperity, room for you and room for me

Children playing happily

No sorrow

No insanity

Just love

Peace, can't you see

A place where we are all free

Oh, what a dream that one day we will all be free

Milk and honey

Grapes too big to carry

More than enough for us all to live

Families happily growing

You and me, oh what a great day it will be

A placed filled with peace and unity

Yet so many people fail to believe

But after living in a world like this

I must believe

I must believe and I choose to believe

There is a better place, another place

It's a promised land

Happily, Ever After

You found me

Finally, we meet

After all these years and all these tears

Praying, waiting and going through the good and bad

Finally, you are here, it's you and me

Proud to say on this day

Your mine, I'm yours, it's you and me

Happily, ever after, we will be

You found me

Finally, searching for so many years and after all those tears

Praying, longing and finally we meet

Going through the good and the bad

Wondering Lord where is she, and God where could he possibly be?

Finally, we meet

It's now you and me, proud to say on this special day

Happily, ever after we will be

The cosmos, stars, universe stopped rotating on its axis as our eyes meet.

Our hearts danced to the rhythm of the heavenly angels and so we both declare on this day

Your mine, I'm yours

It's you and me

Happily, ever after we will be!

Lost Treasure

I found what I was looking for

I found true love

It was sweeter than a honeycomb

Pure as the river and calm as the sea

I found it

What I had been looking for

It was right in front of me

I didn't need to look anymore

No need to search because I found, what I was looking for

Joy took away the pain

Sunshine took away the rain

I found it

All that I had been looking for

It was right in front of me

I had no need to look for more

It was there all along

He was there all along

I found my Savior

I found my comforter

I found my provider

I found my lord

There was no need to search for more

I found my lost treasure

Man, that is good

There are not words to express, just how good

No words to express, how wonderful you are to me

There is not a gift, could even meet the equivalent

Equivalent of your grace and mercy

You are just too good for me

Man, that is good

So good, how the sun continues to shine over me

the sea washes over me

My heart beats and my soul rings deep

Oh, how good you are to me

No analogies or metaphors, could express how much I adore

You are just too good for me

Very good, so good to me

Changing

I'm changing

I don't do the same things I used to

I don't look the same way I used to

I don't go the same places I used to

Things don't even hurt me like it used to

I have let go of the heavy burdens that I used to

Carry around on my shoulders like I used to

I don't even cry the same way I used to because I'm changing

Ever since He gave his life, I'm changing

Ever since He saved my soul, I'm changing

Ever since He opened my eyes, I'm changing

I'm walking different

I'm talking different

My clothes have changed

My heart has been rearranged

My soul is different, and I am changing

Forbidden Fruit

I saw it

My eyes caught hold of it

If only I could grab it

Instantly, I had to have it

Loss of breath and I longed for it

How I wished I could hold it

If only I could taste it

Forbidden fruit, it had me

Forbidden fruit, my soul cries you can't have it, doesn't matter how it looks so sweet

Forbidden fruit, it was drawing me

It looked so sweet

I saw it

My heartbeat grabbed for it

Nice and shiny, glimmering just for me

I had to have it

Not focused on the consequence

Not realizing what would happen once I touched it

Once it graced my lips and I bit into it

I tasted it

Forbidden fruit, it had me

But my soul was crying out,

Declaring you can't have me

Repercussions were too strong

Consequences too strong

Punishment too strong

God's will is too strong

Forbidden Fruit, you can't have me

Yeshua Messiah

Adonai

El-Elyon

God

Savior, Healer, Master, Redeemer

No other name, can save but God

God in the flesh

Emmanuel

Rose of Sharon

Mighty in Battle God

Crucified for me

Hung on a tree

He is risen for me

God

Eyes opened

Heart changed

Mind free, no longer the same

I'm different, so free and happy to say

I'm delivered, eyes open

Heart changed and no longer the same

Eyes opened; heart free

Mind changed, no longer bound to things

Things of the world, things of the flesh

I'm different, so free and happy to say

I'm delivered

Eyes open

No chains holding me down

I'm free and I can see!

Keep

Keep wondering

Keep searching

Would I ever find love?

But my heart proudly sings yes

I have found real love

Keep crying

Keep fighting

Would I ever find love?

My heart declares, yes

This time it is real love!

Keep yearning

Keep learning

Thought this was real love

My heart silently whispers, yes God is real love

Real love died on the cross

Real love was pierced in his side

Real love was ridiculed for me

Real love rose for me

Ocean of life

Keeps crashing into me

But the Captain of this ship is guiding life for me

My Savior, My king

His Hands on the wheel

And with each crashing wave, The Spirit reveals

He is in charge, He's in control

So, I proudly proclaim and won't let go

I'm going to ride the waves, Keeping my head above distractions and beyond the pain

As long as He is with me, I'll be ok

I'm going to ride the waves

Red sea in front of me

Pharaoh behind me

Mountains on the side of me, I can no longer hide

But my Savior is in front ready to ride

Guiding and leading me to the other side

I walk across dry land, as He holds my hand

I'll proudly proclaim and take a stand

I'm going to ride the waves

Stand strong

Hold on

Keep on

Live on and ride the waves!

I'm guilty

I realized that I have put things ahead of you

Placing someone else or something else in the driver's seat

Your hands are no longer on the steering wheel

I hear the tires screech because I'm out of control

How and when did it all begin?

This is what happens when I get ahead of you

I put everything ahead of you

No room for you to move

I'm guilty of an idol mind!

My life spins out of control

When I take hold and force you to let go

Falling deeper in sin

Always losing and I never seem to win

The wound gets deeper

Salt causes my flesh to sting

This is what happens when I get ahead of you

This is what happens when I put everything ahead of you

No room for you to move, I'm guilty of an idol mind

Clean me

Wash me

Purge me, free me

I accept the charges because I am guilty!

I want to press higher

I want to go higher

Insecurities and frailties

Sadly, keep hindering me

But you see the best in me

So, I try to keep my eyes on the prize

Deep inside, I'm afraid and scared

But I hear you say, Let go!

Take my hand, trust me and let go!

I want to go deeper

I want to move higher

Insecurities and frailties

Sadly, keep hindering me

So, I try to keep my eyes on the prize

Deep inside, I'm afraid and scared

But I hear you say

Take my hand, trust me and let go!

Keep your eyes on me

Don't worry about your past, because your new in me

Keep climbing

Keep running

Keep going

Take my hand, trust me and let go!

This time

A lot of times

I come to you, after all that I have done to you

Forgetting that the last time

You took my hand and dried my eyes

And yet I still decide to disobey

And try to hide but Lord not this time

I can't pretend this time

Forgive me this time

It's different this time

I promise this time, it's the last time

A lot of times, I admit

I am mad at you

Like a father, you have compassion for me

I misuse the love, between you and me

But you continue to hold on to me, even after all I have done

And you see the best in me

This time, it's different

I promise this time

Please forgive me this time

I promise and I know I have said this before

But this time, I have made up my mind

No more

I have shed so many tears

Experienced and trembled from my fears

I have been a victim

Been there and done that

But that has changed since I have declared your name

I'm a conqueror

Yes, I am a survivor

I am free

No more chains holding me, because I am meant to win

I don't lose because there is a fighter standing firm within me

So, I fight on, press on, keep moving and stay strong

I have been used and been abused

Ran after things that were no good for me

I have walked through the wrong doors and missed out on open doors, longing for something more

Cried over the wrong decisions and over the choice to open up to the wrong person

Not realizing until it was too late that those people weren't good for me

But that has changed since my mind and heart has been changed

I'm a conqueror

Yes, I am a survivor

I am free

No more chains holding me, and my soul cries out no more

Because I am no longer the same

I have been here before

Feels as though, I'm in the twilight zone

Yes lord

I let you down again, but I still choose to get up again

Tired of living in sin

So tired of how my life has been

Back and forth is how it's always been

Feel like I'm going around in circles

Here I cry again

Feeling misused again and feeling like I'm dying again

Yes lord

I let you down again and I'm tired of living in sin

Tired of how my life's been

Back and forth, is how it's always been

I keep going around in circles

But I must do things different

I no longer will follow my will

No longer living the same

No more living in sin

No need to keep going around in circles

Breathe

Breathe

Breathe in me

Your Spirit

Your truth

Your love

Jesus Breathe my Lord

Take your Spirit and breathe in me

Breathe

Breathe in me

Your peace

Your strength

When I'm alone with you

Your breathe is so peaceful

So powerful

So intriguing

I open up to receive your Spirit

So, breathe in me

Rather have Jesus

I'm not searching for millions and not asking for fame

Just the thought of everyone knowing my name, makes me a tad afraid

There is only one thing I need

Just to have time with my King

You can have it all

I take my Lord

You can have it all

I'll take Jesus

You can have it all

I'll take my Lord

The diamonds and bling

The fame and even the pain it all brings

Have you noticed King Solomon had it all, but was missing an important element?

Where was his relationship with the Most High?

He is an example of someone having everything and yet still not satisfied.

The world can have it all and I'll take my Lord

He wakes me in the morning and smiles down on me making it feel just right

He catches the tears that fall through the night

I smile to myself knowing how good He is

He is powerful and marvelous

Making moves everywhere and yet still has time to tell me He cares

You can have it all, I'll take my Lord

Dry Bones

Can these dry bones live again?

Could what looks dead rise again and live?

Can these dry bones live again?

Could what looks dead rise again and begin again?

Tradition has caused the body to be stagnant

Ceremonies but no power within it

Anniversaries causing the body to be stagnant

Not moving

As it should

But I ask the Lord

Can these dry bones live again?

Could what looks dead rise again?

Tradition has made the Word of God of no effect

So much separation and jealousy within in it

Ceremonies, traditions, anniversaries but where is the power that brings life, love and peace?

Where is the power I read about? Where is the power that I feel so deep within?

But I hear the Lord say, if only we would get out of His way.

Then these dry bones can live again

What looks dry and dead will rise again!

So, we declare and pray for the bones to rise again.

In these times of devastation, Lord we will stand until the dry bones rise again!

Jesus

Jesus

You reign forever more

My heart stands in admiration at the very mention of your name

Jesus

Oh Jesus, my Lord and King

I'll forever proclaim your name Jesus

Forever my lips will utter your name

Jesus

Just thinking of you

How my precious Lord was slain?

For this I give the highest praise

Hallelujah to your name

Oh Jesus

My lord, I will forever adore

My King

My Lord and precious king

Son of Man, seated on the right hand of the throne

Jesus

Where are you Adam?

Where are you Adam?

Did you eat from the tree from which I told you?

Did you think you were bigger than me to take the chance and disobey me?

Can you handle life without me?

Look at all I gave you

I took the dust of the ground and breathed Ruach breathe to birth you

And yet you still chose to eat from the tree

Oh, Adam, where are you?

Physically your standing next to the woman I gave you, you say she is bone of your bone

Flesh of your flesh. You call her woman, I named her Eve

She is your helpmate, but she belongs to me

But you and her spirit are separated from me

We were one, God and humanity

She was deceived but what was your reason Adam?

I gave you power and dominion

I gave you knowledge and wisdom but where are you Adam?

God was physically present in the midst of thee

But Stan surely deceived humanity

It was because of Adams lack of ability to receive the very gifts that God gave to him

He allowed the enemy to separate humanity from God

He lost all of this and he wasn't even hungry

The only way to restore this condition was to reinvent the mission

So, God uses his knowledge and wisdom, even amid humanities condition

He had a solution, so he sent His Son!

I'm broken

I'm open

Just for you Lord

I'm willing to be used for your good

I'm broken

I'm open

Just to be used by you Lord

So, you crushed me Lord so I could learn to be still

And you pressed me beyond measure, so I can learn to hear

You knew I had to be purified, refined and defined

The process was painful, but you were there on my side

You had to break me to rearrange me

You had to soften me, so you could mold me

You had to take away from to add to who I shall be

I'm broken

I'm open

So, you can use me for your good

Travail

My petition

My womb fills with the cries and tears of the children

Nations waring and fighting is ringing loudly in my ear

I can hear the cries of lost souls

So, my heart becomes burden and I cry out oh

Fathers leaving their wives for others

Children killing their sisters and brothers

But I believe the prayers of the righteous availed much

So, Lord I cry save us

Lord save our nation, children and Lord please save us

Laundry Day

Cleanse my thoughts

Cleanse my ideas

Cleanse my impurities

Cleanse my insecurities

Wash over me

Wash me with hyssop and purge me with living water

Cleanse my soul and make me whole

Take out whatever hinders me

Remove what blocks me

Cover under your blood what tries to stop me

Grant me the wisdom to walk away from whatever tries to hold me

Help me to stay clean and pure

Backwards

Close this door for me Lord

Take this bitter cup from me

It's bittersweet to the taste

I should have listened Lord because maybe things would turn out different

There are times I can't go to sleep

The crack from the door shows light of my reality

Please close this door for me Lord

My heart is heavy, my memories dash back to me

But I don't want to go backwards

That's love

Jesus is love, sweet love

Oh, what a love!

Heart broken

Eyes full of tears

I have been yearning and searching for years

Then a still voice, sweetly says come here

Open your heart to hear

Let me show you, what I have been trying to tell you for years

I never knew the true meaning of love

Until I felt his presence from above

Each time I close my eyes

I can feel His smile

So good how you treat me Lord

His love is not puffed up

And it doesn't promote self

His love died for me

Oh, how He cares for me

He was crucified for me, what a love!

The love you bring is life-changing

Oh, what a love

Jesus is love

Can you see it?

Can't you see it?

For I can feel it and imagine looking upon that day

Oh, what a great day it will be!

All worries and concerns are gone away

Yeah

We will be going home

Looking above to the cherubim's flying above me

Worshipping and lifting your name on high

Crying Holy, Holy is the Lamb

What a great day it will be

To know and see that Jesus is standing right in front of me

No more thirst

No more hunger

No more pain

No more rain

Just sun, love, God and His Son

We will even see the one's we lost

Yes, what a great day it will be

Oh, how I wait for the day to go home!

But can you see it?

Changed Mind

You are what you think

If you want to change your ways

You need to change your mind

Be transformed by the renewing of your mind

If your mind is still back in Egypt, then how can you make it through the wilderness?

If you are still enslaved mentally

How can you break the chains physically?

Transform your mind

Transform your thinking

For there lies your power

Your mind continues to be a powerful weapon

Once you get your mind right

Everything will fall into place

The enemy wants to attack your mind

For he doesn't want you to learn how to escape and be free

You are what you think

If you want to change your ways

You must change your mind

Get right or get left

It's time

To get right or get left

Let's be real there is no time for games

Are you hot or cold?

No more time for lukewarm saints

No time for contradictory, hypocritical saints

It's time to get right or get left

Do you want to be left behind?

Gazing at the sky, watching as the saints soar by in the sky

To the place where the Most High resides

So peaceful and lovely

Heaven is the place we will be

It's time to get right or get left

Wake up my people

Time is winding down

No need to pack for this trip, oh just forget it

You don't need clothes for this trip

I don't think you want to be left behind

There will be a time, when even the bibles won't be present

You will need to endure by holding on to His presence and have the word on your heart tablets

Embedded on your hearts for the Word will pour out from the depths of your souls

It's time to get right or get left

Men

Wow

Brothers, Fathers, Sons

You were strategically and divinely created from the dust of the ground

God's fingertips gracefully formed every part of your frame

Then God divinely spoke your name, "Adam"

Brothers, Fathers, Sons

Blessed Trinity looked down upon you and said "this is good"

Let them reproduce, name and have dominion just like Us

And yes, God breathed his breathe into dust and that dust became breathe (Ruach) and that breathe became you.

My how we need you

Wow

Brothers, Fathers, Sons

That means the same power that created the moon and stars

Same power to raise Yeshua from the grave, resides in you

The power that called the sun and skies to form, is the same power that can move mountains and strong enough to start and end wars resides in you

Oh yes Brothers, Fathers, Sons we need you

You have tremendous power oozing from your fingertips, but my heart is grieved because society has labeled you unworthy and only noticed you for your magnificent physique and strength.

But your far more than that, even the strongest of brothers are helpless on the streets with crocheted mats and yet we still need you

Wow

My Brothers, Fathers, Sons

There is so much more to you, power lives deep within you

Male and female classification comes from you

Masculinity and Femininity God pulled from you

My rib is your rib, I was birthed from you

A child's need for affirmation can be negatively and positively affected by you. Men we need you

Wow

Brothers, Fathers, Sons

Same power and ability to move mountains with your prayers, can calm the waves of rage within the

Hears of your sons. Wow, you have power and it reflects in your sons, as they watch you shave your

Beard cut the grass and make momma laugh. Your daughter runs to your arms, because only daddy's

arms can protect her in the raging storm. "Daddy's girl" she proudly proclaims as you sit across from her

3*5 table that barely goes past your navel. Feet uncomfortable, legs too long but you're showing her

humility to get down for a small fake cup of tea. Oh yes, we need you.

Children are watching you and oh be mindful, we children tend to do what you do.

Because again we need you. You're the first example to our sons on how to be a man. You're the

example of when they get old whether they will fall, or will they stand. The first example to a little girl,

how her spouse will be. Will he be a replica of strength or a replica of leave? Oh Yes, we need you. Your

presence matters and God's presence in your life is the matter.

Brothers, Fathers, Sons

Your laugh and intricate knowledge to figure out the mathematical equàtion and divine wisdom to

Protect your family from satanic persuasion, snares and hidden danger. All that is in you. Have you

Fully grasped, what It's like for us to see you? Men we need you

You're surrounded in his Shekinah glory, clothed in royal attire.

Girded in His truth, His love surrounds you and the world trembles in anticipation of you.

Expecting your arrival as prophecy waits for the final feast in the Middle East. We look to you, praying

For the day you grasp the fullness of the wait. How your absence is the weight of a young boy or girl's

Impoverished youth? But how your presence is the long-awaited embrace and words from the Son, well

Done thy good and faithful servant. You are my son

Men

Brothers, Fathers, Sons we need you

Sheepherder

Many vacancies, a whole lot of applicants but not many can handle the job.

The title speaks for itself, many long for it, many fight for it but no many will die for it.

The hourly rate & salary seems good and the benefits seem life changing. The influence is powerful

Atmosphere changing but the responsibilities are self-sacrificing. The sheepherder gathers, watches,

Protect and shears the sheep. So many sheepherders have only focused on the pay and benefits that

While they are shearing, they cut and nick the sheep. Oh, but the pay is lovely and the benefits out of this

world. But the supervisor is watching how we handle the sheep, will it be with pride or love. This position

has many vacancies and a whole lot of applicants but once in the position, they will see how exactly hard

it gets. Sheepherder availability is 24 hours a day, no breaks, no vacays just time spent protecting God's

lambs. Protecting them from wolves, lions, bears, snakes and counterfeits and fakes. Guiding them to

green pastures to avoid unforeseeable chemicals that lie in some pastures.

Cutting off excess fur, so sheep are not blinded by their furry coat. Oh, but the sheepherder must be

very careful when shearing the coat, because if the scissors are too close you can harm the sheep's throat. Piercing areas that only needed to be rubbed. Sheepherder must remain gentle and softly graze

the sheep's skin with love. So, do you still wish to apply? The pay and benefits are good, but the

responsibilities are long. Sheepherding requires time away from the one we love and acceptance to

know some sheep will wander off to other ones. Some sheep will wander off to someone's pasture wishing

for something better, hoping for a Savior but really getting a slave master. Oh yes, the pay and benefits

are worthwhile but the duties are self-sacrificing. Do you still desire the position? The sheepherder doesn't

get to choose which sheep he gets. Some sheep little, tall, stubborn, right, wrong, prideful, arrogant, liars,

lazy oh the list is long. But the supervisor is still watching to see how the sheep are being handled. Will

the sheep be mishandled or treated with love? Again, many vacancies, a whole list of applicants but not

many can handle it. It's a sheepherder that ensures the sheep are red. The sheepherder knows the right

time to feed and knows when the sheep need rest. Sheepherder listens and can discern the cries from

the sheep. The sheepherder holds on closely when they must cross the rivers deep. The sheepherder

remains calm and still when the weather is raging on. Calming the sheep with soft whispers and embracing

arms. So, the position is still available, do you still wish to apply or does this position ignite your pride? You have seen many other sheepherders and you said it looks easy, but most sheepherders have a great

supervisor, so the job looks breezy. So, it is not an easy job they just learned from the best. His name is

JESUS! The great shepherd and He guides His sheep through green pastures, leading the sheep by still

waters. Shading the sheep under tall green trees. Kneeling down close to shear the coat. Spending day

and night, talking to the Father on the sheep's behalf. He is a great supervisor show us that the life long

rewards are far better than salary and hourly rate. No pay can exchange the joy of seeing a lost sheep

return to the pasture. The joy of washing the sheep clean from the remnants of it's wandering. The joy of

hearing a mother and son have reunited. Husband and wife will bring forth life. Dead rising again and sick

children becoming whole again. It far exceeds the salary rate and pay. The sheepherder embraces the

sweat, tears to guide the sheep. Working hard to ensure the sheep are transformed, is his meat. So that

job description is very long but do you still wish to apply? For the duties and responsibilities are long.

Sheepherder must always be wise and never thinking he is big in his own eyes. Humble and kind with a

focus on God's kingdom and lighting darkness with God's marvelous light! Oh, how it brings him or her

freedom. So yes, the position is still available, but do you still wish to apply?

Still here

Before I came to my mother's wound

He knew just what was in store

For me on this earth

Yes, I had some trials

Tribulations, tests and nights with little to no rest

But yes, I am still here

I could be gone a long time ago

But I am still here

My kindness has been used as a form of weakness

My love has been taken advantage

I cried some nights

I felt like I could even die

But this is just a testimony of where I have been

I am still here

I could have been gone, a long time ago

I could have died in my mother's wound

I could have died in the car accident

I could have been dead when bullets grazed past me

I could have died when the love of my life left me

But I am still here

My head is hurting

From the pain and year

The rain is pouring, and I don't know how to keep going on my own

I go on my knees and pray to the Lord

Asking for Him to help me, because I need peace

Peace to stand still

I'm at war everyday with myself

How can I stand still, when I feel like running away?

Lord take me by the hand and hide me in your secret place because I need peace

I never thought life would be this way

I need some clarity and strength to guide me along the way

Lord I need your life-changing, life-altering peace

Some days I don't feel like I can make it

Then I feel this strength come from the depths of my soul

His hand is guiding me

Saying my child, you can

Fly

My child

Fly

My heart is pounding

Feel as if it can leap from my chest

Tears begin to flow from my eyes

I can feel His hands slowly wipe away my pain

He softly whispered

I gave you all you need to fly

I breathed the breath of life

My Spirit is in you

So, my child

Fly

Endurance

I got to keep going and pressing

Have my enemies guessing

Don't tell the right hand, what the left hand is doing

I will prove it to the enemy and tell it all

How I kept pressing and walking through

Each day I must keep going

Trying to figure out what I'm going to do

24 hours of fasting and praying

So, I lean on Jesus and keep saying

Hallelujah Father and Hallelujah Son

The Holy one keeps me going

The enemy whispers for me to give up

he watches, waiting for me to faint

tempting me with pleasures and speaking doubt

But God keeps me going and helps me to endure

The enemy is busy

Using every trick, scheme and demonic tools

Trying to bring up my past and reveal what I used to do

But my Father keeps me pushing and helping me to endure

So, I keep pressing and going because my heart is fixed on serving my Lord.

It is Finished

I'm fighting every day

Fighting at work

Fighting in the community and all around me is fighting

I must keep praying

My flesh keeps tempting me

But I shout with a war cry

For I know it's a trial and a test

These burdens and trials give me strength to press

I must keep on fasting and praying

Leaning on His everlasting arm

Cause I need more power, strength and peace

I can't do it on my own

So, I shout with a war cry

I know it's a trial and a test

The devil is busy

Using tricks and tools and he doesn't seem to quit

So I keep fighting in the spirit of excellence

Because I choose to endure until it's finished

Why do you love me?

After all I have done

Why do you continue to bless me after all I have done?

I don't deserve it

But you continue to smile down on me

Lord why do you love me ?

I'm so undeserving

I'm weak in this fleshly body

Always insecure and not really knowing my purpose in life

But you show me it's alright

I keep my eyes on you

No matter how it seems

God knows exactly how much I can bare and how far I will go

He knows the time that I will be called home

I belong to Him and He loves me

But my heart cries,

Why do you love me?

At your feet

Lay it all at your feet Jesus

Gazing at you surrounded by your infinite wisdom and glory

My only desire is to lay all my burdens, problems and insecurities at your feet.

I don't desire riches, diamonds and land

Even when I'm alone, its in your strength I stand

I proclaim my love for you

I would be just fine for me, to lay at your feet

I could spend all of my life at your feet

Praising your name and worshipping at your feet

My heart beats with joy

All of my mind is focused on your glory

It is a joy just to lay at your feet

There at your feet is safety, joy and everlasting life

For I only desire to lay at your feet

Redemption

Eyes full of tears

As I make my way near to the altar

My hands shake, my heart beats

I quiver, I fall to my knees

Release it all

From the past and what is before me

This is my redemption story

He died for me

His story rings deep

Deep within every inch of me

Hear the nails, I see the thorns

Hear the mockery and sound of His clothes torn

He did it for you and me

Just to tell the world about the redemption story

Darkness falls

Veil is torn from the floor to the wall

He cried just for me

Eli, Eli, Lama Sabachthani

He cried, He died, and He rose

So, we could tell the redemption story

Perfect Peace

Peace something people strive for, long for and many will die for peace.

Hoping to find peace in the streets and only gripping grief. Looking through the yellow pages and skimming through the sections for help to find peace.

Some even jump from bed to bed searching for peace and only end up in pieces. Stripped of their identity, left with uncertainty, believing they would experience peace and are left in pieces. Peace does not come from taking the next hit of the pipe.

Peace does not come from laying next to a warm body at night. Peace comes from giving your life to Jesus Christ. Peace comes when you open your heart and allow God to make it right. His peace is fulfilling and there is no need to be afraid and the currency is your faith.

Faith to believe that even when the world crumbles around you, God has promised his peace. His peace brings you into a full piece. No longer divided, no longer striving, no longer trying to find your peace in man, when your peace is in the Son of Man.

He brings peace when wars and violence arise, you walk boldly through the streets because you know God is on your side. That is the peace He brings when you surrender your heart and mind to the The King.

His peace is perfect, mature, whole, unfailing, never ending, ever lasting and life changing peace. God is and will forever keep you in perfect peace if your mind is stayed on thee.

Clothed in clergical robes, some of their bodies postured from the right and the left. While others are sprawled over due to fatigue from eating last night's offerings. Their shiny gold rimmed plates neatly arrayed with perverse and blemished meat.

Wake Up

Minstrels saturated in glittered linens; mouths open in song but no fire pours from their lips. Worshipping with a strange fire because there is no time for them to consecrate with the Master. Consumed by platform, enthralled with schedules while the sheep are led to the slaughter. Wow look at the massacre. Their furry coat is covered with pride and the minstrels gloat. While the wolf looks on laughing, as he locks on to the sheep's throat.

Wake Up

Apostles are increasing in number, but their drink offering is contaminated with arrogance and clutter. They make no room for God to come through and the wind is not behind them as they pretend to move. The position has consumed their passion to seek God and His heavenly throne. Their mind has become consumed with how many sheep are now his or her own. Pushing an agenda that is not supported by the Father. Slowly turning around grinning with pride because of all the sheep that follow them.

Wake Up

Saints continue to fill up their plates layered with all the fixings they adore. The shepherd is pouring out God's Holy writ, His word. But they spit out the meat because their glued to their seats. Gagging on the Holy meat and choking on the milk. Longing only for the materials, soft linens and royal silks. Prestige and acknowledgement, not realizing it's making them spiritually sick. Vomiting up the Word of God as it passes through their system, never making its way down to the root. Their ears tingle longing to hear a word but they rejected it's fruit. Their bellies full of dextrose sugars, unnatural and contaminated rivers. Trees debilitating from the root. For the rivers they are planted near are fed by a bitter root. Their attendance is increasing and the Pastor smiles looking on but he or she fails to see that their light is no on.

Wake Up

The clock keeps ticking and Satan keeps grinning. For he no longer sends devices when saints remain divisive. Belly full of gossip, slander and lust. Portals flooded with social media, Instagram and Facebook while their spiritual body longs to be fed from the Holy Book. While others read their word daily without fail but they refuse to apply it and it's only leading them closer to hell.

Wake Up

Our children are disinterested in listening to what we teach, because as they walk through their home. They hear parents don't practice what they preach. Their vulnerable and impressionable souls are being taught by the streets because we have become timid. Afraid to address the real issues they face, so we lead them through dangerous traffic, as they teach themselves how to navigate through the streets. To busy feeding another's child while your own is left to figure it all out. Their child-like faith, wavering from the hypocrisies that have been witnessed. Steady hearing the preacher say come home but our lives do not match the Throne.

Wake Up

It's getting closer to the time. The witches and warlocks have gathered in size. Violence and death saturate the planet but we focus on the wrong things consumed by a sandwich. Wow sad thing to know we would rather feed our flesh. Then lay it all down at the altar and confess we are a mess. Admitting we are shiny sparkling dirty cups. For we need to open our hearts to allow God to clean and fill us up. For a broken spirit and a contrite hear, He wont despise. But what does He see when He looks at us with His all-knowing eye? We can sense the oncoming of the rapture but He left us with talents, don't forget about His pasture. So get up from your slumber! There are too many things to do and so many lost souls that can't be numbered in need of you. So sons of God arise for it's time to eat. Take each page from the Word and digest it's delicious meat. Wake up, arise for it is time to spread the gospel of Jesus Christ. For soon the trumpet will sound and He will appear riding on a cloud.

Wake Up

The wall is solid and strong, wide enough for the king's chariot to ride on. The watchmen's height is too short to climb or to stand on but spiritually we see beyond the walls to know what is going on.

Our sleep is interrupted to pray for others, we march in the spirit, while others lie peacefully under the covers. Our orders from the Savior is to pray, some things we don't understand. But we know our Father and He knows the heart of man. We are the Watchmen!

We can sense the oncoming of a storm, so we warn the shepherd to protect him or her from harm. Our feet are laced tight with the gospel of peace, we must remain filled with His glory, so we can see spiritually the plans God must reveal. He speaks through the night, that it is time to wake up. Sending us to stand firm and sound the alarm. Warning our brothers and sisters that the witches and warlocks are rising up. We sound the alarm for the saints to prepare for war. Standing firm at the city gates, to prevent the enemy from coming through the doors. Stepping in to intercede for another that has been harmed, while the other watchmen cover us from the flaming arrows that seem to swarm

The arrows blot out the shade, but we know our Father and He knows the outcome of this day. We are the Watchmen

Back straight from the load that the watchmen carry but reading His word, is what keep us merry. Helmet of salvation keeps our minds sharp because we block out the enemies whispers and self-sabotaging thoughts.
Breastplate of righteousness protects our heart of flesh because if not careful our heart can lead us into a mess. For we can't be led out of emotions because we must guard the wall, for if we moved by how we feel, it could injure one or maybe all. We must stand guard with the shield of faith because there will be things that will try to cause us to waiver in our faith. We are the Watchmen!

We walk in integrity and speak in truth because our belt must stay on, and we quickly warn our brothers when their light is fading or when others is not on. Our necessary food is the word for it provides us strength and endurance to press on. The word brings us hope as the world seems to grow cold. We hold on to his instructions and stand guard fully arrayed in our armor to share His word. We stand guard, ready for what is come but we don't fall or

faint because the battle is already won. Interceding for leaders young and old, telling them of what is to come. For they all shall behold His splendor, His majesty, the greatness of that glorious day. When every knee will bow and every tongue confess that Jesus Christ is Lord. We are the watchmen!

So we continue to work while we wait, for he left us with instructions. When He tells us to go right, we follow because our reward is to please Him. We only desire to serve the Master. The job never gets too hard because God provides us with all we need, as we stand guard to warn His sheep.

We continue to pray for the brethren for what may lie ahead in the day but confident in knowing that our Lord will make a way. We continue to watch both night and day, for we know the enemy is waiting for a small gap in the door to enter the city gates. Our spiritual binoculars looking beyond the trees the shadows, keeping an eye on any movements that are not the character of our Master. So while we work, we wait for He left us with instructions. We always follow His lead to remain free from corruption. We are Watchmen!

Invitation

The sonic wave is pulling you closer, the Spirit is drawing you much closer. Sending out the signal that it is time to come. Oh, wandering sheep you have strayed for too long.

Can you feel the drawing that it is time for you to come home?

As you cried out through a thousand thread count sheets, I heard you and came quickly but you failed to remain within my reach. I sent an invitation, but you failed to reply.

You preferred to be cuddled and enabled but my invitation was sent to heal you from inside. As I warned you of the enemies' devices and taught lessons that would make sense.

You were more drawn to flattering words and snuck off beyond the fence. Oh, wandering sheep you have strayed for too long.

Can you feel the drawing that it is time for you to come home?

You question if I am real because life seemed to be full of pain, that was not a part of the deal. The more I remain quiet; your thoughts began to riot.

But my dear child, I was teaching the importance of trusting me in the silence. For I witnessed the injustice, inequality and pain. I saw how the rich got richer, and the poor get poorer and how rain could not wash away the pain.

I sent an invitation, but you refused to reply. I warned from the beginning and instructed you with my word that man's days are full of trouble, because of the disobedience that occurred. But my Son died for it all, so that we will be in tune.

In tune with His rhythm and His will. I have sent the invitation and there is time for you to apply before the deadline. So come to Jesus, while there is still time!

Come to Jesus, so the true you can be revealed, and your inward man can heal!

Additional Poems From The Heart

Renewing our Vows

It flashed before my eyes, the picture of our union. How I shopped for months looking for the perfect gown. Making sure I was adorned with jewels and a crown to lay humbly at your feet. Totally prepared and ecstatic for what was to come. You courted me for years, gently inviting me to your secret place, where you and I could abode. Hidden under your wings in pure and unadulterated love. You welcome beyond the chambers to see your face. I was overcome with emotion that I vowed to remain faithful to you until death. It was the sweetest thing to watch you humbly get down from your heavenly throne to die for our love. It was a beautiful moment of bliss, a time that I did not realized I missed. I became enthralled with busy schedules and routines, that I failed to you provide you with what you desired. I gave you crumbs from what was left of me and expected you to embrace it, because at least it was a small part of me. Something is better than nothing, right Abba? No, I was wrong, and I thought you had left me but really it was I that slipped to the side. It was your daughter that became distracted by the whispers of other suitors, who were dressed in designer suits but were ruthless looters. Looters sent to steal, kill, and destroy our bond and union between one another. It all flashed before my eyes and I realized that I was wrong, and you were always right. I had to decide to repent of my ways and return back to my groom. As I knocked on the door your heart, you graciously let me back in. Washing me with the word to remove all the blemishes and dirt from within. The word cleansed me of wickedness and evil that idolatry brings. Putting their flattery ahead of your warnings, was a sign of the deep-rooted sin within. Disobedience brough discord to our union and wanting to be accepted left me broken and wounded. But yet you cleaned me up and gave me back my crown. We began to talk again, laugh again and we began again. Each day you courted me, as if it were the first time we met. Your warm embrace and unmerited grace. My and my first love reignited again for once and for all. I told my other suitors that I have returned to my first love. There is nothing or no one that can love me like my Father above, my king and my first love.

Divine Persuasion

My soul longs for you

As my heart beats for you

Our love has ignited and my spirit desires to behold your glorious face

I am persuaded

I can't be contained, for at the mention of your name I humbly bow

Willingly praise

Proudly proclaim that at the mention of your name, nations will bow

We humbly bow, our spirit bows to your name

Open and willing

Ready to serve for your words are written and hidden in my heart.

There in the deep chambers of my heart, your mysteries are revealed

I am persuaded

I can't be contained that at the mention of your name I humbly bow

Willingly praise

Proudly proclaim that at the mention of your name, nations will bow

We humbly bow, our spirit bows to your name

There is none higher

There is no one bigger for you are the one and only God

There is none higher

There is no one bigger for you are the true and living God

I am persuaded

I can't be contained that at the mention of your name, I humbly bow

Willingly praise

Proudly proclaim that at the mention of your name, the nations will bow

We humbly bow and my spirit bows to your name. Your love has me divinely persuaded to remain under your wings of grace and mercy!

Who am I?

you are the light

in the darkness

you are the peace

in the midst of storm

you're my strength

when I'm so weak

you give me life

when I can barely breathe

who am I?

that you are mindful of me

who am I?

that you think of me

you are the light

in the darkness

I cannot hide

even though I tried

there you stand

Holding out your hand

you are my strength

when I'm so weak

you give me life

when I can barely breathe

how you love me

despite my deeds

ask you for more, you give me bread

ask you to change this and you give me living water

ask you for strength, you give me joy

ask you for peace, you give me life

you restore the time, and replenish the years

Who am I?

That thou are mindful of me

Who am I

That you think of me?

#RealTalk

Intimate conversation between Father and daughter

God can I get a manual for this thing called life?

The gospel music group, "Mary Mary" had a song on their album that I played on repeat daily. Listening to every high note, rip, run and octave change failed to prepare my heart for the weight of this world. Carrying it on my shoulders did no justice to the scars that were left from piercing stings and daggers of injustice. The song would play continuously on the radio, hearing the melodic sounds of Tina Campbell & Erica Campbell declare "no one said the road would be easy, but I don't believe He brought me this far to leave me". But, as I remembered the song from the early 2000's, now I was in my thirties. I responded to the song as if it asked for my approval. Well no one said it would be this hard! Speaking from a place of devastation, disappointment and discouragement, instead of a place of gratitude and solitude. Recalling the beautiful memory of being cocooned in the fluids of my mother's womb. If only we could return to the warmth and comfort of being connected to the umbilical cord of simplicity. I thought to myself, God a manual would have been great. One would think once we exit our mother's wound and feel the slap of the doctor's hand on our bottoms. A brightly laminated manual would appear with instructions on what life will bring, how to react and respond to the unexpected events of life. Unfortunately, I would learn there is no manual, but we do have specific instructions on how we should live according to God's Holy writ. We have God to guide us along the way. He is a great Father and for this I give Him praise. A survivals manual sounded like a great idea until I turned 37 years old. But God did place a manual in the Earth for His people. It is the Word of God! In the pages of scripture are countless nuggets of wisdom, that address the daily problem's we face. Everything we face and how to face it, is in the Word of God. It's in the Word of God that our Heavenly Father reveals His heart to us. It's in this very book that the dim flame in our hearts can be rekindled and enflamed. It's His Holy Word that planted its seed of new beginnings, transformation and renewal. It's in spending time in God's Word and speaking His Word back to Him that I was able to overcome depression. So no, God didn't grant my request for a manual given by doctors at a child's birth. But we have the greatest gift and guide, the Holy Spirit. We have the Father and when life blows its blistering winds and torching flames. We can proudly proclaim that we won't be shaken by every wind, rain and storm. We have God and that is all we will ever need.

As I sit and reflect on the many occasions that a manual would have been beneficial. It was in September 2011, Tropical Storm Lee hit and Harrisburg, PA was flooded with rain. Sitting in Wednesday night bible study hearing the teachings of my grandmother. I said farewell to the saints and drove home, completely unaware of what would occur in a few hours. After a hard day's work and bible study, I was knocked out. Until I awoken from my sleep to the sound of rushing water. My bed was close to the sliding back doors, so I looked out from the covers and saw nothing. So, I got out of bed and felt cold wet carpet. It was then that I noticed the waters were flooding through the apartment. Completely panicked, all reserve and poise left me, and I was hysterical. I don't remember if I called anyone, but I do remember grabbing my Louis Vuitton duffle bag. I placed a few personal items into the bag and then heard a knock at the front door. It was the River Rescue with a boat in front of the house. It felt like Noah's Ark had physically manifested in 2011. I told the River Rescue team, No! I am walking through this water. Not realizing that the water was full of the unimaginable things because it was pitch dark. Only flashlights, a red boat and figures from nearby neighbors could be viewed. I just took the man's hand and quickly walked through the water. The water was waist high, but I didn't care, my focus was to get as far away from the water as possible. Once I reached higher ground and quickly calling my mother to tell her that I would need somewhere to stay. Then it dawned on me that my car, Pontiac G6 which I lovingly called "Big Black" was parked in the back. Once I walked back down to get a visual of the damage to the car. It was clear that "Big Black" was surrounded by water and all I could see was the roof of the car. There I stood no house, no car and a lightly filled Louis Vuitton bag.

After taking two days to find a storage, contact insurance and I was able to return to the apartment. Once I returned to the apartment, all that was before me was destruction. The apartment was covered with bugs from the river, shoes were all over the floor, leaves and branches decorated the apartment to reflect the damage of Tropical Storm Lee. After evaluating materials needed to prepare to move all items into storage. Returning to place all the items into bags and put into storage, I arrive to all my items placed in the middle of the apartment complex. Standing there in shock, completely confused because I was just at the apartment to check all that was needed for the movers. My kitchen items were gone and all that was left lied in the middle of the apartment complex. I cried because this made no sense God. Rent was paid and yet my items were thrown out after just being a victim of a natural disaster. Totally shocked and I contacted my mother, uncle and his friends. They helped me get the items to storage and I went to my mom's house and just cried in my little sister's bedroom. It was during this time of stripping away of all I held dear, that I realized who was really with me and who was for me. It took everything in me, not to feel that life was pointless during this time. At the time of the flood, I was married. Even surrounded by family, friends and loving coworkers to provide support, life seemed pointless. No one would ever know until they read this book, that I wanted to end it all. My ex-husband during this time was out living his best life in the club, while I was trying to pick up the pieces. It was during this time that I realized things must change. God knows His daughter, so He came to me in a dream. Showing me exactly how I felt and that there would be glory after this. So, through all that was being revealed in those around me that crushed my heart. It was in those moments, that God's word became my food.

Aww, Man I really wanted those throw pillows!

So, I know you're probably wondering, what does God have to do with throw pillows? Well, let me explain and you will see the correlation. It had been years since we had new furniture. I was looking on Facebook marketplace to determine if I wanted to decorate with vintage pieces or get a brand-new set. Contacting several people about Queen Ann chairs, ottomans, sectionals and chaise lounges. I was determined to makeover our living room but to no avail nothing caught my eye. So, after reviewing several options online, my husband and I decided on a grey sectional with yellow and brown Aztec pillows. One day, while shopping with my mother there were two yellow printed throw pillows. I was so excited and searched the entire store looking for a second set. To no avail, I left the store with one set of yellow throw pillows. For months, I had been looking for this exact set of yellow printed throw pillows. Months, when I say months, I mean months. Unrelentless searching and searching to find the exact match. It was so dire to have yellow throw pillows that I almost bought a yellow pair, but it wasn't a match! Major emphasis on not a match.

After giving up on searching for the exact match, I went shopping for a ball gown at one of my favorite stores Ross, Dress for Less. After fitting my ball gown, I walked past the home and furniture section and my eyes beheld the beautiful color of yellow. Dashing quickly over to the printed yellow throw pillows, I realized it was the one's I had been obsessed about for months. I smiled and when I got up to the register, it hit me. What if I would have bought the mismatch set out of impatience and would have been disappointed?

Disappointed that I bought something mismatch just because it was the color, and I wanted it that bad. It took me back to October 2014, when I fell madly in love with a former coworker. Completely awestruck by this man and couldn't wait to see him, when it was time to go to work. He sat and ate lunch with me, even defended me when I was insulted by another coworker. Totally in awe, when he brought me soup when I was sick. But never once did he express his feelings towards me. I was going back and forth in my mind about him being my ideal guy. He was cute, successful, well-known in the city of Harrisburg, but he never expressed the same feelings I had. I would talk with my coworkers about it and people thought we were a good match. It took a hard realization when I found out he began dating a coworker that I thought was my friend. What hurt the most was the fact, that I told her that I really like him. It was in that moment, that she made her move. It crushed me, totally disappointed and the friendship he and I had, changed tremendously.

I kept hoping and believing, it was just a fling and our friendship would reignite again. Nope, I was completely wrong. It was a whole year later until I finally felt bold enough to talk with him about what happened. Again, searching for something and hoping I would find it. Then it took a dream from God for me to finally wake up and realize this hope in being with my coworker, wasn't an exact match to the plan God had in place. Completely consumed by my emotions that I failed to see things from God's perspective. Failing to even take the time to learn this person's faith in God or lack of faith. Let's be honest ladies, many times being with anybody feels better than being with nobody. We make these proclamations and create unrealistic lists of characteristics and features desired in a man. He needs to be 6'5, tall, dark, handsome but after countless nights spent alone. We start crossing certain items off the list and end up with people that are completely mismatched. We tend to ignore our lists and fall head over hills in love with the closet suitor. Then we become upset with God when the pattern we created doesn't quite fit in the fabric! It is important to learn the beauty of waiting patiently for God to send the right match! It was quite some time before I found the correct color and design of the throw pillows. But trust once the match was found, it looked perfect in the living room! It was in that very moment that I had to give God praise for his timing and superb design abilities. God is a master builder, architect, designer and homemaker. He knows what should go where and what pieces brighten up the room. He will always make the right selection and knows what pieces match. We just have to be willing to wait patiently, while He puts the masterpieces together.

It was August 18, 2018 when, God put the pieces of the puzzle together for eternity. On this beautiful Saturday in Niagara Falls, New York in front of fifty of our closest friends and relatives. I married David Schyler Washington, my sweet, loving, kind, gentle and protective husband. He is the right match! We are not perfect and who is perfect but Jesus Christ! But I know for sure that he loves me, and I didn't have to call friends and family to crack a Morris code to find out. He shows it in his love, touch, conversation, laugh and the way he looks at me. If you look in my husband's phone, you will find so many pictures of me. I crack up laughing and tell him that he is going to run out of space with these photos. But I wouldn't trade it for anything. God was perfect in His timing to bring us together. We first met at Cheyney University in Fall 2000 and only shared a kiss. Only saw him a few times and then we loss contact for 15 years. It took 15 years and a failed marriage to find the perfect throw pillow! Trust my hubby is a comfy pillow and he is always there to comfort me.

Daughter, you need a heart transplant!

The heart is an organ that pumps blood throughout the body via circulatory system supplying oxygen and nutrients and removing carbon dioxide and other wastes. The heart is the size of a large fist with an average weight of 10-12 oz (288 grams-340 grams). The sole purpose and function of the heart is to structure electricity and plumbing. The heart has four chambers which include two upper chambers (atria) and two lower chambers (ventricles). After studying on heart transplants, I had a few questions to ask Abba. Lord there is nothing wrong with my heart! It pumps and beats correctly. What and why would I need a heart transplant at such a young age? It's not your natural heart but your spiritual heart needs a transplant! Also, you must be willing to sit down to heal from the heart transplant. I was completely confused, and it took some time to realize what ABBA was lovingly telling me.

Matthew 23: 25, "Woe unto you, scribes and Pharisees, hypocrites! For ye make clean the outside of the cup and of the platter, but within they are full of extortion and excess". When I read that scripture, I had to admit that I felt convicted. Convicted because first I didn't want to be a scribe, Sadducees or Pharisee because they murdered Jesus. But God was telling me that internally I was far from Him. I knew some of the Word of God and was getting by with those that saw me externally. But inside God saw that my heart was completely broken. It can be difficult to hear that you're not as perfect as you paint yourself out to be. God is merciful, loving and true and if you're willing; He will show you the true you! I started doing research and learned that Heart transplants occur because the heart has become diseased and needs replaced with a healthy heart.

It was during my research that I looked up the causes and effects of a diseased heart. After recognizing the tremendous effects heart disease has on the natural body. I understood why ABBA was adamant about me getting a heart transplant. But not only was having a spiritual heart transplant important but the rest is just as important. I was always busy doing something for the Lord or so I thought it was for the Lord. Singing with local gospel artists, groups, choirs, being an extra in music videos and meeting different people around the city. I was just busy and not about my Father's business. Not realizing that after I go home to be alone, there my heart was silently breaking and breaking into pieces.

Years of heartache and devastation couldn't be drowned out by people's acknowledgement, affirmation and praise. It all was dung in the eyes of God. If I died in that condition, I was not going to heaven. I would be going to straight to Hell because my heart was not right. It was on the surgical table of my surgeon Dr. Jesus that I had to lay prostrate for Him to cut me open. Oh, but the only difference about this surgery, there was no Novocain. I felt every cut, pulling, breaking, sewing, moving, redirecting and shaking in the process of surgery. Even though I felt the pain of the procedure, I began to learn about God's perfect peace. The word of God speaks about perfect peace, "Isaiah 26:3, "You will keep him in perfect peace, whose mind is stayed on You, because he trusts in You". It's His perfect peace that the pain was bearable, and the discomfort was eased. The Holy Spirit kept me during the toughest process of the heart transplant. God had to remove all the disease parts of my heart and create in me a clean heart. King David would declare in Psalms 51:10-12, "Create in me a clean heart, Oh God and renew a right spirit within me. Cast me not away from thy presence and take not thy Holy Spirit from me. Restore unto me the joy of thy salvation and uphold me with thy free spirit".

I feel my brother when he wrote this beautiful song to the Lord of Lords. I can't go on like this Father because I don't want to wound your people with my mess.

Sacrifice was required in this process and things that I held dear, had to be cut away. I loss my stepfather who suddenly died from cancer. Family members and friends became distant and I felt like an outsider. Finally realizing, the breaking, tearing and rearranging of my life was revealing God's perfect plan. So, it took some time to humbly accept the need of a heart transplant. But to know that ABBA was directing the procedure with His loving, gentle and wise hands, helped ease the fear. Helped ease the fear of being completely relinquished of my inhibitions and insecurities. God showed me the beauty of letting go and to embrace the sharp scalpel that leads to recovery and complete wholeness.

After the transplant, the process of resting was difficult at first because I was so used to being busy. I had to learn how to sit still, learn to tell people no, create healthy boundaries with people in my life. In the time of rest, it was when I learned the beauty of being planted. In the book of Jeremiah 17:7-8, "Blessed is the man that trusts in the Lord and whose hope the Lord is. For He shall be as a tree planted by the waters, and that spread out her roots by the river and shall not see when heat cometh but her leaf shall be green; and shall not be careful in the year drought, neither shall cease from yielding fruit".

It was in the time of rest that I felt like a tree planted by rivers of living water and I knew it! See at times, many of us declare that we are free, liberated, changed but our actions speak that we don't believe. Our actions continue to speak bondage, fear, depression, oppression, rejection, etc. When we receive Jesus Christ as our personal savior, our lives should be transformed. But don't get me wrong, there is a daily death to our old selves. It was not easy hearing from ABBA that my heart had become contaminated. With the many experiences I have faced from childhood to know, I see how it became contaminated. But the Father didn't want my heart to remain contaminated and he doesn't want yours either. Just as King David requested for ABBA to create in him a clean heart; we must do the same. I had been lying to myself declaring that I was this tree planted by the rivers of living water, but my tree had been uprooted. God had to uproot me from the familiar and place me in unfamiliar territory to reveal His plan. It's not easy walking in the unfamiliar. It causes the mind to want to gravitate back to the familiar. To be honest, some of us do go backwards because we fear the unfamiliar. The unfamiliar places teach us that we must fully depend on God. We must depend on God to endure, press and fight the good fight of faith.

So no longer was I comparing my life to others and devaluing the uniqueness of who I was in Christ Jesus. There was no need to rush the journey because the other trees around me had full flowers, when I was only budding. I was at a place of acceptance and appreciated the time of rest. The time of rest, when the Holy Spirit would provide water and nutrients necessary for me to grow. A joy to accept and allow my thirst to be completely quenched by reading God's word. At a place of stillness and rest, where I didn't' need to respond to every rustling and bristling wind that would call my branches to bend. I am grateful to be able to feel the wind blow and still stand under the SON and not the sun. The uprooting from the familiar to unfamiliar was for sure a open-heart surgery. It required healing to take place to allow the undetected areas of my heart to be renewed, revived and refreshed. My only focus during the spiritual transplant was to be content. Content in the aspect that when unexpected storms, winds, rain, snow and rising currents from the raging waters; I won't be moved! I will be content and not moved, choosing to remain completely at peace in God's perfect will and perfect peace.

Stop trying to prove who you are and just be!

It took a long time to know that I was accepted by God. Because for quite some time, I was long for acceptance from people. I don't share this story but to those near and dear to me. But it was difficult accepting that I was different. Fitting in to crowds, clicks and groups was never my strong suit. I was cordial, polite and sociable but fitting in seemed to always lead to disaster. Just when people seemed to like me, boom! There was this switch that took place with those that I was longing to fit in with. There attitude would change, or they would become distant. I began thinking that I was the problem and whenever meeting new people; I would fight to prove that I am a good person. To be honest, it was draining. Trying to prove who you are to people depletes your strength, time and life. It's also a form of idolatry. When the Lord revealed to me that longing for acceptance from man was idolatry, I was convicted. Whether you are a theologian, new convert or seasoned saint, we all know idolatry is an issue to God. God's first commandment clearly states in Exodus 20:3, "Thou shalt have no other gods before me". (KJV). Trying to prove and find myself by fitting in and longing for acceptance from people was idolatry. It was idolatry because it became a God! Sometimes we think a god(s) are only golden statutes, figurines, cards, stones but many of our god(s) have two legs. Some of our god(s) are tall, dark and handsome but deep inside they are as dead bones. Many of our god(s) are material possessions, status, prestige, degrees, accolades, acknowledgement and money. I was one who searched, yearned and longed for acceptance and that became my god. See when you are so consumed about being heard, seen, acknowledged and placed on a platform before others, that my friends are god(s). Many of us are more consumed by filling a void that we focus more on the creation and not the Creator. My need for acceptance came from countless numbers of time that I faced rejection. Growing up in a single parent home until I was nine gave me my first lesson in rejection. My father was not around and so I longed to be in his presence. For him to see me ride my first bike, tie my shoes, receive honors on my report card, etc. There were countless moments that I longed for him to be in my life. I had heard about his involvement in other people's life, but longed for him to be in mine. It took me 36 years to finally leave that longing to be accepted by him at the altar. I honor him for being chosen to be a part of God's plan to bring me here, but he was in God's hands. God was showing me how far and deeply rooted this issue of acceptance had reached.

Abba knows the very core of our existence and the issues of life that we failed to heal or address. God showed me how I was trying to prove who I was to my family, church and job. Pushing myself to the limit and being a yes person was leading me deeper and further into idolatry. As a worshipper, it is important to worship in Spirit and in Truth. As written in John 4:24, "For God is a spirit and they that worship Him must worship Him in spirit and truth" (KJV). Our hearts must be pure in our worship and service to God, so we can be a sweet aroma to his nostrils. 2nd Corinthians 15:2, "For we are unto God a sweet savor of Christ, in them that are saved and in them that perish" (KJV). To learn that searching and yearning for acceptance was idolatry, I had to repent because my heart was not pure. Therefore, if my heart is not pure then my worship is as dung unto the Father. So grateful for God's grace, because He is gracious to reveal the error of my ways. So on my honeymoon vacation in November of 2018, me and God were able to reconnect on the sea. As my husband and I were sitting on the top deck of the cruise ship, there stood the moon. I just gazed at it realizing just how wonderful God is and that the moon doesn't need to do anything but shine! The moon doesn't have to perform, act, cry out for attention and acknowledgement. The moon comes out at the proper time and the proper place because of God's word. God told the moon to shine so many years ago and still to this day, the moon continues to shine. The moon does not have to prove that it is the moon. People from billions of miles away know it is the moon. Nations that speaks different languages all know and recognize the moon. So why do we need to prove ourselves? God created us from the dust of the ground and formed us in His image. God is not walking around trying to prove to people that He is God. He is God! There is nothing that needs to be proved because He is the Truth!

I had to look up the definition of acceptance, when God revealed that I was operating in this mind set. According to Webster's dictionary, acceptance is "the action of consenting to receive or undertake something offered" and "the action or process of being received as adequate or suitable"

http://www.merriamwebster.com/dictionary/acceptance

(After time of prayer, reflection, transparency and deliverance, God revealed some key points about being me! It took a long time to embrace the real me because of my longing for acceptance from man. I love converse sneakers aka chucks and a tutu skirt. I will wear a tutu and some chucks so quick because that is me. Whether I am at church, home, work or in the community, I love to wear some chucks. This is the part of me that is different that God has helped me to embrace. It's not about the tutu or sneakers, it's about the freedom of embracing my uniqueness in the Kingdom of God. There are so many believers that are entangled in the prisons of people's expectations and views of them. But there is beauty in being who God called you to be. When you know your accepted by God, you don't have to prove who you are! Let your life speak for you. While away on our honeymoon in a moment of transparency with ABBA, I asked the Lord to show them who I am! I asked this because I was no longer, yearning for acceptance from man and was no longer trying to prove who I was to man. If someone thinks a certain way about me, let them think it but I am not going to prove who I am. Because proving who I am to man was only leading me down the path of destruction. It was liberating to be free from people. I think many of us need to be delivered from people. Delivered from their opinions, ideas and misconceptions of who we are. When you know your accepted by God you embrace being peculiar and you stop worrying about image!

We live in a society that is consumed by image. Look at Instagram, Facebook, twitter, television, movies and magazines. Everyone can be filtered, edited, resized and cropped out to paint a picture of perfection. With the perfect phone application, one can add filters to make their size 24 body slim down to a size 4. There we are trying to fit in to a society that is not authentic or real in the first place. So, our genuine selves have now become ungenuine because of our desire to fit in and be accepted. It is a beautiful thing to be you and a treasure to know that we are peculiar. When you know your accepted by God, there is no need to fit in or compete. How can I serve the people of God, if I'm trying to be a carbon copy of someone else? How can I serve like this? How can I lead like this? How can I grow like this? Being honest and real with God required some deep questions to be answered.

I needed the Lord to wash me with His word, purge me with His Spirit and for the Lord to do a new thing. Lord even if doing a new thing hurts, just do it because I want to serve in the Kingdom of God, completely whole! So, I knew God had graciously healed me from acceptance because things began to change in my life. So, pointers of knowing for yourself that you are accepted by God. When you know your accepted by God you remain committed to His will and obey His instructions. When you know your accepted by God, you glory in your weakness and not your strength. Apostle Paul stated in 2nd Corinthians 12: 7-10, " because of these surpassingly great revelations. Therefore in order to keep me from becoming conceited, I was given a thorn in my flesh, a messenger of Satan to torment me. Three times I pleaded with the Lord to take it away from me. But he said to me, My grace is sufficient for you for my power is made perfect in weakness. Therefore I will boast all the more gladly about my weaknesses so that Christ's power may rest on me. That is why for Christ's sake, I delight in weakness, in insults, in hardships, in persecutions, in difficulties. For when I am weak, then I am strong" (KJV).

Apostle Paul was helping a sister out in this scripture. Because he was keeping it real when he wrote to the Corinthian church. Knowing you are accepted by God, helps you embrace the insults, hardships, persecutions and difficulties of life. When you know your accepted by God, you can't wear someone else's armor. Growing up in the local church it seemed the whole town knew my family and that creates pressure. Because many times we keep the children in a box, not allowing them to stretch out and be there genuine selves. People would see me and say your Mrs. Bonner's daughter or Pastor's granddaughter. I would say yes but my name is Latoya. Being Mrs. Bonner's daughter or Pastor's granddaughter is a role and I am honored because they are family. But that is not all that I am, there is more to me. So it created pressure because being out in the community, that is what people would see that I was the daughter or granddaughter and not Latoya. Proving who I was came by singing at events and making a name for myself. Making a name for myself was not done with malicious intent but God showed me that it was me longing for acceptance. I had placed my identity in the hands of man. It's dangerous to place your identity in someone else's hands. Because if their perception of you changes, then you start questioning who you are and that my friend's is too much power for someone to have. You begin to question if your anointed, gifted, called or chosen because others have shaped who you are. That is too much control and power to give anyone. You make that person an idol because their perception, view and idea of you is more important than being who God says you are. You become more concerned with how others view you instead of how God sees you. I couldn't live or serve like that! God showed revealed intimately that I was accepted in His eyes. Totally and completed accepted by God. Every flaw, insecurity, doubt, fear and quirk were accepted by God and covered by the blood of the Lamb.

God, this is not what I Had in mind

Summer 2016, I had officially been employed for ten years and was ecstatic. Having been blessed to have experience in current and old processing systems. I felt it was time to apply for upper management. Even my current supervisors and managers, had encouraged me to apply. I felt it was the right time to move up the corporate ladder. Even though both my Bachelor and Master's degree, were not necessary for the position. I thought it would be an added bonus for the powers that be, to view on my resume. I realized that too late, that there was a scheduled day off for me. But I refused to take that day off and reschedule my interview for another day. Instead I was dressed for success, wore my best outfit and even spoke to Abba deeply that morning. I was ready for the three-point shot on this interview. Practiced all the potential questions of course. For example, why should we hire you? What are your five best and worst qualities about yourself? I was ready, completely trained, equipped and ready to present myself as the best candidate for the position.

Arrived early and waited patiently to be called in for the interview. Once inside the room, the two managers said thanks for coming in on your vacation day. I just smiled, because thinking yes, they noticed my dedication and commitment to the organization. After at answering and asking pertinent questions about the position. They informed me, that they would be in touch for a possible second interview. After waiting patiently over the weekend, arrived Monday morning to see that I advanced to the next step. I was so excited, yeah God this is it. I calmed down, didn't want to seem to cocky or arrogant, but I just knew this was it. Everything I dreamed and worked hard for was now getting ready to happen. It was down to two candidates, me and another fellow. I was so nervous, because there was a third interview with the Big Banana or whatever they call it. I just was completely nervous, talking to Abba again and again about making a way for this position. Then it hit, my intuition started to kick in and I noticed how people were acting. I thought I was losing my mind, but I just felt in how they were acting towards the other candidate that I wasn't selected. But, refusing to be impatient, I waited for their email in regards to the selection. Then I arrived to work on Friday, and noticed a celebration going on in the other candidate department. It was then that my countenance completely fell and I'll admit I was crushed. But choosing to still be optimistic and not assume. I waited for the email, which finally arrived Monday morning. We have chosen another candidate that better fits the position. Unfortunately, due to the lack of experience in this one area, we have chosen this person.

Politely thanking them for considering me for the position, but inside my spirit was crushed. This is not what I had in mind Jesus! See, what others didn't know is that since 2012, I had applied to over 100 jobs. Even going as far as to travel to Wilmington, North Carolina for a job interview. Only to be told that I was over qualified. OQ, is basically the polite way to decline an individual for a position. Hearing those words more than thirty-times, created a space that I didn't know existed, regret!

Not shortly after being turned down from the position, another opportunity arose to apply again. But this time, I refused to give all of me in the interview. I became numb and refused to even pretend, to want the position. Even the interviewer, said I have heard so many good things about you but I'm disappointed. I wanted to say to the interviewer, no I am disappointed. Do you even know my story? Do you even hear the no's that I have heard over the past four years? But, four years later, it was evident the no's I heard was God's protection. For little did I know that being in upper management, meant having more problems. Oh, I may have been focused on the money, but what about the issues that arise as a result of managing people. Didn't biggie say that, more money more problems! Flashback of my teen years, sorry. After wallowing in self-pity for months, I started to hear from God about what felt like rejection. I took the denial so personal and failed to see God's shield of protection. It took four years to recognize how ungrateful, I had become toward my first love. See, I prayed to God for this job and then complained because I wanted more money. But in those ten years, and now thirteen, He shielded me from several layoffs, management, and staff changes. It was His shield of protection that was keeping me from potential health issues that would and could arise with work-related stress. It was His love, that helped me to see that He knows what is best. If I would have been selected for the position, I wouldn't have time to do what I love. I wouldn't have had the energy or strength to fulfill my duties in the Kingdom of God.

See, God knows that sometimes I pile multiple tasks on and then complain it's too much to do. But God, was merciful and His no was only protection. So, instead of complaining about what should of, could of or would of. I chose to be open to see what God wanted to show me, through this process. He revealed an ungodly desire to prove who I am to others in my family and community. He revealed areas that needed to be mended and whole in order to be fruitful in the Kingdom of God. Unrealistic expectations of people and sadly, myself. Putting time restraints on my life, as if I'm God. No, I am not God. God is in complete control of my life. He knows what is best for me and He holds my hand. One of my favorite scriptures speaks so eloquently about God's love and consideration for us. Psalms 8:4-6, What is man, that thou art mindful of him? and the son of man, that thou visitest him? For thou hast made him a little lower than the angels and has crowned him with glory and honour. Thou madest him to have dominion over the works of thy hands; thou has put all things under his feet.

The scripture continues to encourage my spirit, each time it's read. God, thinks so highly of us, that He is mindful of us. I am on God's mind and so are you! We are on God' mind, and so even though I was turned down from the job. God didn't turn me down, instead He showered me with continued mercy and grace. Now four years later, what I once had in mind is not moving up the corporate ladder. But to seek God's face and dwell in His presence. Money, fame, recognition, and acknowledgement is not on the forefront of my mind. But God, saying well done thy good and faithful servant, Matthew 25:23.

What I had in mind, was not pleasing to the Father but pleasing to self. I'm so grateful that God sees the whole picture, while his children seem to focus only on the frame!

ABOUT THE AUTHOR

Deaconess Latoya Washington is a woman after God's own heart, she is a skilled poet and writer, but also an amazing worshipper.

She is the daughter of Veeta Bonner and Cornell Corley but raise by her mother and stepfather Jimmie Bonner.

She is a Harrisburg native and a Harrisburg High School Class of 2000 graduate. Graduated from Elizabeth town College with Bachelor of Arts in Criminal Justice. Master of Arts degree in Human Service and Counseling. Currently work as a Clinical Specialist serving individuals diagnosed with Intellectual Disabilities and Autism.

She is married to David Washington a Philadelphia native and co/owner of Rhema Creationz. A small black owned business that sells t-shirts with a biblical message.

They are currently serving at Elevated Life in Christ Community Church in Harrisburg, Pennsylvania.

To connect with her, please see information below:

WEBSITE: www.rhemacreationz.com
EMAIL: rhemacreationz@gmail.com

Made in the USA
Middletown, DE
31 August 2020

17038398R00060